Thanks for the Memo

Recollections of Fence Houses, Lambton,
Burnmoor, Chilton Moor, Dubmire & Bankhead

by
Lena Cooper

Fence Houses Junior School, 1949, Class 5. Back row: Kenneth Beedham, Fred Hall, Brian Lister, Peter O'Shaunessy, Harry Thompson, Tommy McKitten, ? Iveson, Harry Baines, Jackie Bainbridge. Third Row: Miss Davison (form teacher), Ralph Oliver, Norman Walker, Margaret Dodds, Maureen Davison, Jenny Thompson, Jean Hackworth, Freda Bolton, Harry Graham, Brian Williams, Mr Kirkbride (headmaster). Second row: Brenda Stark, Phyllis Ann Smith, Norma Wilson, Nancy Wears, Hazel Hill, Marjorie White, Mary Callender, Sonia Gardner. Front row: Ian Sinclair and unknown.

Previous page: Fence Houses Modern Under 14s football team, 1958. From the front: J. Moore, R. Laverick, R. Patterson, J. Weeks, C. Hill, C. Richardson, G. Tiplady, J. Bainbridge, K. Brown, J. Slack, C. Clish and T. Keating.

Royalties from this book will go to Cancer charities.

Copyright Lena Cooper 2008

First published in 2008 by

Summerhill Books
PO Box 1210
Newcastle-upon-Tyne
NE99 4AH

Email: andrew_clark@hotmail.co.uk

ISBN: 978-1-906721-07-7

No part of this publication may be reproduced, stored in a mechanical retrieval system, or transmitted, in any form or by any means, electronic, mechanical, photocopying, recording or otherwise, without prior permission of the author.

Introduction

In this book are many memories of my birthplace, Fence Houses and the neighbouring communities of Lambton, Burnmoor, Chilton Moor and Bankhead. Alongside these memories are rare photographs that capture life in the area and I am very grateful to the many people who have been kind enough to share these cherished images with us all.

The memories cover my life up until the beginning of the Second World War. Times were hard and money scarce, but we survived due to the spirit of the people.

Memories are precious gifts. Enjoy the book.

Lena Cooper
Fence Houses, 2008

I dedicate this book to the memory of my beloved grandparents
Thomas and Dorothy Bulmer. Without whom I would not have survived.

Here are a few lines from a song that puts into words the feelings
I have for my grandparents:

Pal of my cradle days
I needed you always,
Since I was a baby upon your knee
You sacrificed everything for me.
I stole the gold from your hair,
I put the silver threads there.
I don't know any way I could ever repay
Pal of my cradle days.

Lena Cooper with some four-legged friends.

Acknowledgements

Lena Cooper acknowledges with gratitude and sincere thanks the following people for their contribution in photographs and encouragement to the compilation of this book:

Geoffrey Berriman, Alan Brett, Lilian Curry, Brian Dixon, Fred Ellison, Bob & Connie Garden, Margaret & John Harland, Paul Lanagan, George Nairn, Cyril Rickaby, Sadie Scott, Shirley Shields, John Slack, Ann Sowerby
and Edith Winter (née Hardy).

Very special thanks are also due to Norman Walker and publisher, Andrew Clark.

Appreciation and many thanks for co-operation go to:

Beamish Archives – The North of England Open Air Museum
Sarah Stoner – North East Press Ltd, Sunderland Echo
Tony Henderson – The Journal

An advert for Houghton Engineers Ltd, on Dubmire Trading Estate in 1950.

A multi-view postcard of the Fence Houses area.

Back of Beyond

Dear Village – now known as 'Back of Beyond'
Where those small wage packets
Hid such big hearts, as men lost sweat
And blood to raise energy's warmth
While women worked and prayed for peace
But no work now for either young
Or old. A has been! A never was!

Yet once – with Christian folk who truly
Cared not for themselves but for their
Fellow men – was so alive, with
Coaldust covered streets, with daisies
And buttercup gold in green fields
Plus kindness – always with kindness
In gruff voice they gave thanks for what
They had not, then so gladly shared
With all their friends – the mite they had.

When will your heart beat strong again?
And mirth peal forth from youths and men
Rejoicing in a work-filled scheme,
With faith and hope in man's lost dream.
The dreams that live in every heart
Will come to life – just make a start
By asking blessings from above
And sprinkle them with lots of love.

Dear Village – you'll rise with glory
When all folk who live your story
Say 'Back of Beyond' makes us sore
We'll change that name for evermore
And give our village back its pride
In love and care – that nearly died.

Life At Home

I was born at my grandparents' house in Woodstone Terrace, Fence Houses two years after the end of the First World War. For reasons I was not aware of until much later in my childhood, I was brought up by my Grandma and Grandpa Bulmer (my mother's parents). Mother had developed Tuberculosis and died on Christmas Day when I was seven months old.

Grandma's house routines were really organised. Monday was always washing day and quite hard work for the females of the family – two aunts were still at home and not yet 'married off'. When I was much older I tried to use the poss-stick to put pressure on the clothes which were already soaking in the wooden tub. Even though I could just lift the poss-stick I could not put any pressure on forcing it down on to the wet clothes. I never tried again.

Invariably, the next process of the washing episode was drying, then ironing – there were a lot of clothes to do. I did manage to be able to iron a couple of handkerchiefs but no more because the iron had to be fire-heated when it grew cold and I was wasting the heat of the iron. Thank goodness someone invented the electric iron by the time I grew up and of course electric washers.

Happy days of my life were rare because my grandparents were quite strict disciplinarians but looking back now I thank them for it.

Grandma's cooking skills were brilliant. Money was scarce – after all they were both on a pension and they had me to look after. I remember suet pudding, mince pies and Yorkshire puddings. There always seemed to be lovely food for me. One day I constantly looked forward to was Thursday because that was baking day with bread, teacakes, pies, buns, sometimes a custard tart, smaller jam tarts and occasionally a plate sponge cake or queen cakes. Of course this produce had to last the family for quite a while or at least until the next baking day.

One of my aunts got a job at the local brickworks so for a while the budget was increased. However, not by much because she had a boyfriend and I believe that marriage was on the agenda.

My other aunt contracted Tuberculosis and died at the age of 26. She was my favourite aunt and I was very upset. I had lost the one person who in my childish mind had replaced my mother. In my early years Aunt Gladys was always there for me and I felt that she loved me, just as I loved her.

Gertie Dawson with poss-tub and mangle at Lambton in the 1930s.

My arrival on the scene in 1920, followed by my mother's death on the Christmas Day of that year, must have caused my grandparents loads of problems and worries. They had brought up their own family that as far as I can recall consisted of seven girls and two boys. All except the two aunts at home were already married and in their own abodes.

As I was nearing school age (5 years old) it was decided that the family would move to Briarwood Street, Fence Houses. The houses were owned by the colliery (as most houses were in those days) and of course Grandpa was a retired miner. Most of the street had sequence numbers (as in 1, 2, 3, 4, 5, etc) but on the opposite side to the front gardens they were already building New Briarwood Street. The top half of Old Briarwood Street had baths in but the bottom half up to Number 10 had no baths. All of the New Briarwood Street houses had baths. The numbering of the two streets was changed and the New Briarwood Street took the odd numbers and the Old Briarwood Street took the even numbers. So our Number 9 became Number 18.

My Aunt Gladys at Wolsingham Sanitorium with Grandpa in the 1920s.

The reason given to me for the move was that it would be much easier for me to go to school than having the longer journey from Woodstone Terrace. The school was just at the top of Briarwood Street. It sounded like a good idea when it was explained to me and it worked out well.

In the new house that we moved into we still had to have a fair-sized tin bath which was half-filled with 'bearable' hot water and on a Friday night I had to be given a bath in front of the fire by either Grandma or one of my aunts. A coal fire was really warm to my childish naked body. I never knew when the grown-ups had their baths – I would most likely be in bed. So Friday night for me was bath night then always a clean night-dress to go to bed in; 'feeling brand new'.

To me at five years old everything was an excitement. I had to make new friends and start learning how to behave in company so life took on a new meaning for me. I was given little jobs to do at home to help Grandma and, on reflection now, everything that happened to me had a purpose.

At the bottom of Old Briarwood Street there was some land that was turned into what could be called allotments – not very many though. As my Grandpa was a retired miner he got one of the allotments to grow vegetables and I think he later kept pigs. I do remember near to Christmas people ordering their meat from him (I think it was pork) and the parcels of meat having to be delivered for each order. Needless to say our Christmas dinner was pork, stuffing, Yorkshire puddings and green vegetables from the garden, including Brussels sprouts, turnip, carrots and potatoes.

One thing that I never forgot was to always be sure that Christmas was a very special time and it was important that there was food and maybe home-made ginger wine to celebrate that special day. As a child, if I woke up on Christmas morning and found that the stocking I had hung on the brass line under the mantelpiece the night before was heavy I knew that Santa Claus had called and left in my stocking an apple, orange and half-a-dozen monkey nuts. I was overjoyed.

Days To Remember

Every year on 5th November was always remembered with a bonfire, crackers, roasted potatoes and lots of fun. This applies to most of the country and dates back to Guy Fawkes. My earliest memory of Bonfire Night was when we lived in Briarwood Street and the bonfire was set up in 'The Rec', opposite where we lived. I had never before seen hand-held sparklers whizzing round and round and looking like a million mini-stars. Rockets whooshed up and away tapping eternity's doors with their noisy exits.

While bonfires' flames seemed to almost touch the moon and potatoes were cooking on the hot ash of the fire, the smoke-drenched air was stifling to our young lungs but what fun.

I remember an occasion when Sir Alan Cobham brought his National Aviation Day displays to a large field opposite the Dun Cow Inn at Primrose Hill. It was generally known as 'Cobham's Flying Circus' and it toured the country. We were fortunate to be chosen as one of its venues. I was taken to see this display of aeroplanes and it was so exciting. Aeroplanes! We had only ever seen aeroplanes flying in the sky. This was in the 1930s and before the Second World War so I was very impressed.

When the Chapel held its Harvest Festival it was really lovely. All kinds of vegetables, flowers, and fruit were on display, most of them donated by local people in support of the Chapel. I used to wonder where did everything come from – I was too young then to realise the goodness in people. It was such a lovely sight.

The last time I said my 'piece' at the Chapel Anniversary Day I was still quite nervous but managed to hide that feeling. We always were given a prize after the Anniversary Day and on my last time with the Chapel – before starting to go to church – I was presented with my prize. It was a lovely book entitled *Granny's Girls*. Really appropriate, I thought.

I loved the excitement in the build-up to Christmas as a child but as I got older it took on a different aspect for me. In my heart I harbour a strange view about it and the reason is that deep down inside I knew that my Mother died on Christmas Day.

The Christmas of 1937 was also a very sad time for me because my beloved Grandpa had died just before that time. But Christmas is a celebration that we should enjoy and be happy. I admit that now in my later years I love to see people, especially children, enjoying it and having fun. Remember that life is for living not moping.

Another day to remember was again around Christmas time and a very good male friend at the time bought me my first pair of fur-backed gloves. I was absolutely thrilled. My first pair of fur-backed gloves! Now that was a day I could never forget. In my eyes it was like a gift from heaven. I had never been used to gifts of that nature in all my young life. They were such a luxury. I was almost afraid to wear them in case they should get mislaid and someone should maybe steal them!

Grandma Bulmer in the mid 1920s. She died in 1933.

When I was at Fence Houses Infants School (before I sat the 11 plus exam for to go to Houghton Grammar School) every year on 24th May we all celebrated 'Empire Day'. This involved the children having a very enjoyable time at Morton House (home of a very important mine owner). At least I should say on the beautiful lawn in front of the large residence. We danced around the Maypole, all of us representing an Empire Day country – these were countries who were members of the British Empire (Australia, Canada, New Zealand, etc.) To us young folk it was exhilarating and enjoyable and definitely a day to always remember.

Dancing around the Maypole in the 1950s – not in Fence Houses but another Durham village.

Another day I remember always was when I was into my teenage years and 'nearly' but not quite yet 'grown up'. We had some good neighbours always and our neighbour in Briarwood Street will never be forgotten by me because one Christmas she gave me a present to signify my acceptance as a grown up by her at least – a pair of silk knickers! Happy days.

Lena Cooper in happy mood post war.

Grandpa Bulmer in the front garden of 18 Briarwood Street in the 1930s.

Pictures of the Past

A postcard view of Station Avenue, Fence Houses, in the early part of the twentieth century. At this time sending a postcard, often with a local view, was as common as sending an email or text message today. In 1900 over 400 million postcards were sent in this country. By the end of the First World War this figure had doubled.

South Crescent, Fence Houses around 1922.

Above: Station Avenue, Fence Houses. A postcard sent on 30 December 1909. The message reads: 'Wishing a very happy New Year.'

Right: The back of the above postcard. The postmark: 'Fence Houses Dec 30 1909'.

A postcard produced by Robert Johnston of Gateshead from around 1912. Each of his postcards had an unique number and it is possible to date his cards by these numbers.

Schooldays

At the age of five I was taken to Fence Houses Infants School at the top of our street and registered as a new pupil. After I got settled into this school life I began to really like it. When I first started we had a lovely headmistress. Her name was Miss Potts. She was nearing retirement age and was succeeded by another lady named Miss Woodward who was a firm believer in school discipline and used the cane to enforce this. However, she was fair-minded and I think we respected her for that.

We played the usual games in the schoolyard at break times, running around and enjoying the fresh air. In the winter when there was frost or snow we used to make 'slides' over the covered ground. It was while sliding like this that I fell and fractured my left elbow. This involved having to go to Sunderland General Hospital for x-rays and further treatment. This accident affected my future working life as a nurse in my late teens and early twenties. It affects me more and more now as I get older and nothing can be done because of age.

In 1926 there was a General Strike in the country and some of the schoolchildren were allowed free soup. I was not, the reason given apparently was that my grandparents were not eligible for this concession as only the children whose fathers were involved in the strike were considered.

Miss Woodward of Fence Houses School in 1930.

I was entranced by all the things I had to learn at school and with the encouragement of my beloved grandparents I really tried to do my best. The result was that I passed the 11 plus exam and was accepted to attend Houghton Grammar School. This changed my life and I look back on those schooldays with great feeling and pride. In many ways Houghton Grammar was a new way of life for me. So many new things to do and so many new subjects to learn – some of which I had never even heard of. The headmaster was Mr Jones and the senior mistress was Miss Shallcross. It seemed to me that the only actual contact with these two would probably be if a student had done something wrong. Although of course they would be visible at the morning services or they may have been noticed walking along the corridors of the school on various missions.

A typical group of youngsters in the 1920s – these children are from Dubmire School.

Because of my injured left elbow I was excused some of the outdoor exercises such as hockey and other games but I was expected to do the indoor exercises that I could do. Our physical training teacher was a Miss Thompson and she was terrific in all the things she showed us how to perform. It was almost as if she had 'rubber bones'.

The school uniform for girls was a medium green tunic with wide pleats front and back from a basic top and red sash type belt to fasten at the waist. The outfit was completed by a white, long sleeved blouse with a green and red striped tie, stockings and black shoes. The boys also had the white shirts with the same tie to go with their suits. The boys had green caps while the girls had green hats and both had the school badge on the front.

While at this school I knew that I wanted to become a nurse even though I was aware that I had to reach 18 years before I could apply for this. It was my life's ambition. It was at the age of 13 that I lost my best friend – my beloved Grandma who died from cancer. I was completely gutted. I felt so lonely now with no Mother, no Aunt Gladys and now no Grandma. I was approaching the threshold of womanhood without my loved ones. Everyone was sympathetic at the time but no-one could ease the pain of a young teenager who had lost her lifelines.

As time moved on my Aunt Lena and her husband John and their young son Denis got our house put into their name and moved in with us. It was a wise move because Grandpa was failing in health as well. One of Grandpa's friends suggested to him one day that there was a vacancy at the Co-operative Bakery in Chester-le-Street for a young lady to work in the office and he indicated that I should apply for it. I was at that time not quite sixteen but I was told to apply for the job. Money was scarce and I was now needing more grown-up clothes. I had no option but to go for the job. I still had some months to do to complete my term at Grammar School so I was convinced that I would not get the job but to keep the peace I applied. Well I couldn't believe it but I got the job. So permission had to be sought from the school so I could leave before the end of term. However, I was granted permission to leave under the circumstances. So that ended my schooldays and started my working life.

A class from Fence Houses School from July 1931. The picture is damaged but it is worth including to remember everyone who is featured on this school photograph. Mr Gledhill (headmaster) is seated far left, behind him is Mr Cameron and seated, far right, is Miss Scott.

Dubmire Junior School class, 1947. Back row, left to right: Mr Greenwell (headmaster), ? Cresswell, unknown, Frank Sykes, Christine Powney, Doreen Robinson, Mavis Berry, Mary Tindale, Kenneth Cope, Donald Batty, unknown. Middle row: Jimmy Southern, George Gaunt, Charlie Taylor, Brian Knight, Clive Taylor, Tom Bell, Raymond Archer, Gordon Williamson. Front row (seated): Marjorie Bell, Iris Bullen, unknown, unknown, unknown, Maureen Hamilton, Audrey Wood and Mirian Fenwick.

Fence Houses Junior School, 1951, Class 3. Back row: Ian Sinclair, Brian Lister, Jackie Bainbridge, unknown, Fred Hall, Peter O'Shaunessy, Brian Williams, Kenneth Beedham, Jim Southern, Mr Kirkbride (headmaster). Middle row: Harry Baines, Freda Bolton, Tommy McKitten, Norman Walker, Jenny Thompson, Harry Thompson, Ralph Oliver, Jean Hackworth, Davis Caldwell, Leslie Langley. Front row: Phyllis Ann Smith, Sonia Gardner, Maureen Davison, Nancy Wears, Brenda Stark, Mr Gasgoigne (form teacher), Moira Bilton, Marjorie White, unknown, unknown and Hazel Hill.

Dubmire Junior Mixed School, Class 1, 1950.

A group photograph of a number of male pupils of Fence Houses Secondary Modern School around 1954. They are at an unknown event but all the pupils are dressed. Back row, left to right: unknown, Anthony Mallaburn, Norman Walker, Alan Richardson, Maurice Curry, Billy Charlton, Chris Pigford, Mr Clark (teacher). Third row: Clive or Geoffrey Gardiner, Donald Gardiner, Eric Hill, unknown, Thomas Elliott, Ken Joyce. Second row: unknown, Brian Lister, Alec Chaplow, Arthur Stavers, unknown, Trevor Pattison. Front row: unknown, Malcolm Allison ?, Trevor Marshall, Ronnie Burns, Billy Enright and unknown.

Teaching staff from Chilton Moor School, 1917. Mary Hardy is shown seated on the front right. This photograph was on the front of a postcard which she had addressed to her brother Tom who was stationed in France with the DLI during the First World War.

A class of girls from Chilton Moor School, 1920. Unfortunately, only one name is known and that is Elizabeth Howe who is third from the left in the second row.

A group of children from Fence Houses Junior School around 1950. Back row, left to right: Donald Gardiner, Norman Walker, Harry Graham, Barry Hackworth, Eric Hill, Billy Wilson, Mr Kirkbride (headmaster). Third row: Brenda Lister, unknown, Valerie Hutchinson, Violet Ridley, Maureen Davison, Sheila Twinn, Moira Bilton, Jean Willis. Second row, seated: Margaret Dodds, Jean Anderson, Marion Tate, Doreen Tindale, Joan Mills, Marian Iverson, Jean Willis. Front row: Elizabeth Swan, Peter Bell, Geoffrey Gardiner, Brian Lister, Clive Gardiner, Ralph Oliver, Maurice Ramshaw and Mary Callender.

Pupils from Fence Houses Modern School on holiday after the Second World War. The youngsters stayed at a camp at Kessingland in Norfolk. Behind them you can see the old army barracks where they slept on soldiers' bunks. On the left is headmaster Mr Gledhill who retired in 1953.

More pupils from Fence Houses Modern School on holiday at Kessingland in the 1950s. Second on the left is headmaster Mr Gelson.

Childhood Games and Memories

When we were young, but of school-age, there were a lot of games we could play in the backstreet. A very popular game with us was known as 'hitchy-dabbers'. It involved marking on the ground a group of sections to represent an 'aeroplane' (that's what we called it). The 'dabber' was the base of an ordinary jam-jar. This was sped along the ground to reach one of the 'sections'. Then the person whose turn it was had to hop on one leg to reach the dabber without stepping on any section outlines, pick up the dabber and hop back to base. Everyone tried to be a winner and there were many laughs.

There were always games with ordinary skipping ropes and this involved one person at each of the rope ends to turn them for us to jump in and skip, then out without getting caught in the rope. Trying to catch us, sometimes the rope-turners speeded it all up by turning the ropes quickly.

Tops and whips were another popular game to play in the street. The tops were patterned with coloured chalk then spun on the ground and the whip was used to keep it spinning.

Blind man's buff was fun up to a point but there had to be several players. There were a number of other games that we played as youngsters but as we got older we looked for other activities.

I remember also as a young person I must have done something wrong because I was sent to my bedroom as a punishment – it was early evening in the summertime. I just sat on my bed and looked out of the upstairs window. After a short while there was a tap on the window and a clothes prop appeared with half a turnip stuck on the other end. I opened the window to get the turnip and waved at my friends who had made sure I was not going to starve. Funny how I never forgot that incident.

Playing on the swings – Sadie Slack in 1940.

The first time I was taken to Houghton Feast I was sure that this was 'another world'. My mind was filled with the excitement of roundabouts with music, swings in boats, dodgems, sideshows and just about everything you could imagine that would impress a young mind.

Left: The Houghton Feast fair held in the Market Place in the mid 1950s

Right: The fair at Houghton Feast in 1963. In the foreground are the children's favourites – shuggy boats.

I always liked the cinemas in both Houghton and Chester-le-Street and would go to one or the other according to which film I wanted to see. At Houghton there was the Coliseum, further up the street was the Empire and next door was the Grand. All of them had good films and it was sometimes difficult to know which one to go to see. The decision was often made according to available funds. The same principles applied with regard to Chester-le-Street which had three picture houses. The Empire, which stood a little way back from the main street, was also used for ballroom dances which were very popular. Further down the street, and on the other side of the main street, was the Palace, a popular picture house. At the bottom of the main street and to the left was the Queen's picture house which was also very popular. So we were spoilt for choice. The only thing that made our decision for us was the total cost. In both Houghton and Chester-le-Street it was not only the cost of admission but also the bus fares involved to get there. We had to accept the fact that if we had not got any funds then we couldn't go but we could dream couldn't we? We believed the day would come when having enough funds for our entertainment would not be an issue. In our young minds we would get a job with good wages and have money to spare!

Left: Inside the Empire Cinema in Houghton in the 1950s. Twenty years earlier seats on a Saturday night were priced 3d to 1s 3d. Still expensive to youngsters with very little money.

19

When We Were Young

Edward Walker (left) with Raymond Darby (right) and an unknown girl at the bottom of The Drive, Fence Houses in 1941. The two boys are in their Houghton Grammar uniforms. Raymond Darby was an evacuee with Mr & Mrs Walker of Sydney Street for the war years.

Norman Walker and Brian Williams in their Lambton Cub uniforms up The Drive, Fence Houses.

Above: A street party at High Row for the wedding of Prince Charles and Lady Diana in 1981.

Left: A Christmas party at the Bursgreen factory (formerly Houghton Engineers) in 1975.

In the backyard of a miner's cottage at New Lambton in 1959 are John Harland, Alan Weeks, Thomas Harland and Anthony Smith.

Betty Pratt about 12 at the Rec in the late 1940s.

Edith Hardy outside the front of 17 Station Avenue North around 1941.

My Early Working Life

When I got my first job at the Chester-le-Street Co-operative bakery department I thought I was to be working in the office. I was not aware that this was only to take telephone orders from the Co-op branches around the area for their bakery requirements that day. This information was then taken by me into the bakehouse and given to the foreman baker for him to allocate the work to his other bakers (two of whom were female). As soon as the orders were completed and packed on to wooden shelf-like containers they were then ready for collection by the bakery van men who would deliver them to the various branches.

My starting time was 6 am at the bakery but as the local buses only started their day at 6 am I had to walk three miles to get to the job on time. Luckily, I was able to get a bus home at the end of the shift – between 3 and 4 pm.

After taking the day's orders to the foreman baker I spent the rest of the day working in the bakehouse – greasing tins, washing up constantly and any errands that had to be done. There were other girls working there who had more interesting work but I was the junior.

As time went on I was allowed to service the tea-room that was below the bakehouse and had its entrance door facing the main street. (The tea-room was also Co-op property.) It was for to help shoppers to have a break with a sit-down, a cup of tea and maybe a biscuit or teacake. This was where I learned how to make a pot of tea and how teacakes were toasted.

In a matter of months we heard that the bakery was closing down and we would be transferred to other jobs within the Co-operative stores. I was lucky enough to be transferred to Fence Houses Branch drapery department. This meant for me a starting time of 9 am and only a few minutes walk to work. It was before the store was reorganised and each department had its own entrance door. There was a great amount to learn but I had a very nice boss, a Mr Ted Phaup, and the travelling salesman, a Mr Tom Jefferson, helped me a lot!

Fence Houses Co-op after modernisation when the departments were combined.

If I worked there till I was 18 years old then I reckoned it would be time to apply for to become a nurse. I made no secret of my ambition so it came as no surprise when the time arrived for me. (The international situation at this point was very uneasy.)

I had to have three references to support my application for a nursing vacancy at Preston Hospital, North Shields. I got one from the Reverend A.J. Gadd (our local church vicar), one from Mr Young (manager at Fence Houses branch of the Co-op) and one from Alderman Peter Sargent (a longtime friend of Grandpa's). After an interview I was accepted for probationer training initially.

To say it was a totally different way of living could be said to be an understatement. However, I was so determined to become a nurse, nothing would stop me. Even then I had no idea what the future held.

In September 1939 war was declared between Britain and Germany and everything changed. The patients were transferred to a hospital in the country and away from the perilous coastlines of North Shields. This was to be sure that all beds in the wards would be available for wounded servicemen. This happened sooner than any of us expected and in a very short time the ward I was on was full of ill or wounded, or effected in some way, servicemen. I remember one morning walking down this ward at the beginning of my day's work and I could see the faces of these young men looking at me – some with tears, some with sad looks, some with half a smile, some who couldn't see me for bandages, some who said 'Good morning, nurse,' some who slept and one who winked his eye at me. When I returned to the duty room I knew that helping to get people back to health was so important to me.

The probationer nurses lived in the nurses home with a night nurse calling us up in the morning in time to be on duty as the night staff finished their shift. This meant we could never oversleep because invariably the nurse involved called your name to make sure you were awake and left your bedroom light on. Incidently, the living part and the bedroom part were all in one room.

We then had to wash, get into uniforms including the head-dress, and make our way to the canteen for breakfast then report for duty to our wards, usually to the ward sister or staff nurse who would then allocate your jobs for the day.

Once in a while we were sent to work on other wards to gain further nursing experience. I remember one time I was sent to the maternity ward. Another occasion I was sent to the children's ward. I loved it all. There was a shortage of nurses at the beginning of the war years and sometimes I was in charge of a ward on night duty.

Lena Cooper in her nursing days.

One incident comes to my mind whilst working on the children's ward on night duty. A young child died. In those days we used to make a gown of white lint and sew up the sides so that a child's body could be decently covered before taken to the mortuary – a kind of shroud. This was my first encounter with the death of a child and I was breaking my heart as I sewed this garment for the child. When night sister called to check all patients she caught me in tears. She told me to report to her in the morning, at 8 o'clock, before going off duty. I did so and she was so kind to me. The words she gave me and her advice have helped me for the rest of my life.

Mining

A busy scene of industry with Lumley Sixth Pit in the background. Note the full coal trucks and Wood Row behind.

The underground pit pony stables at Lambton D Pit in the 1920s.

Officials filling duff for the power station at Lambton Railway during the 1926 General Strike.

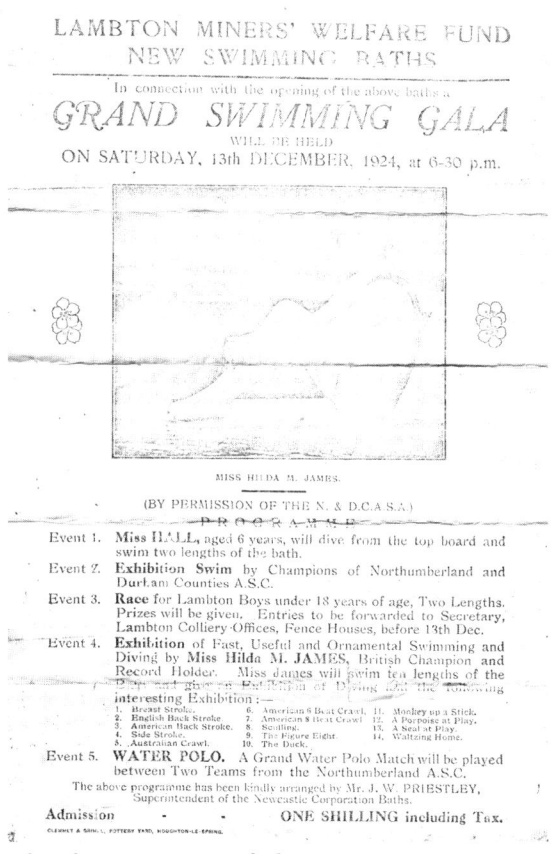

The front cover of the programme produced when Lambton Swimming Baths was opened in 1924.

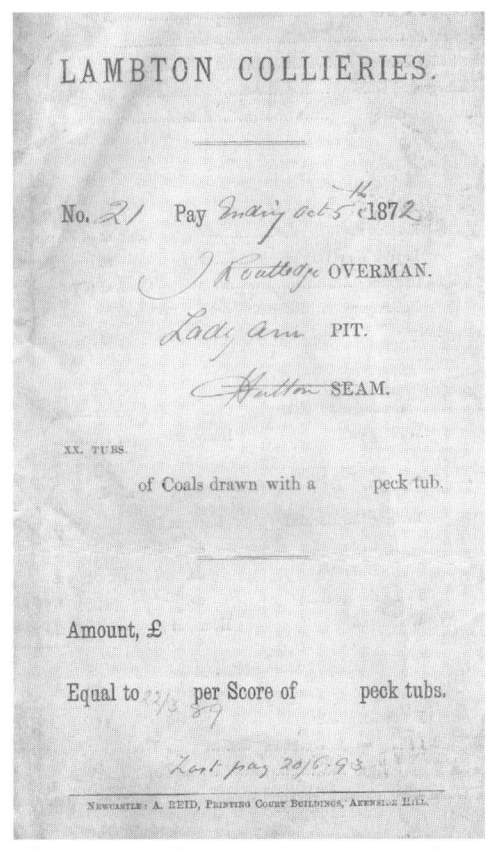

The cover of a rare document that gives an account of work wrought out of the Lady Anne Pit in 1872.

Transport

Mr John Elliott Snr with his son John Jnr from Fence Houses. This photograph was taken in 1927. John Snr worked at Lambton D Pit for a number of years before working at Joplings in Sunderland. John Jnr also worked at Lambton D Pit. Both Johns were keen footballers and both played in goal.

Fence Houses Station in the early 1960s. Note the piles of parcels and sacks on both sides of the platform. The station was demolished only a few years after this photograph was taken.

A tram makes its way along Station Avenue, Fence Houses, around 1912. This is another postcard by Robert Johnston of Gateshead. The number of the postcard shows that this photograph was taken at the same time as the one on the bottom of page 11.

An engine at Lambton Coke Works filling with water. The water was softened to take out any lime. This engine was built in 1912 and was in service for over 50 years before being scrapped in 1970.

Lambton Cokeworks

A busy scene at Lambton Cokeworks that employed many local people over the years.

Terrie and Marion – clerical staff at Lambton Cokeworks in the 1980s.

The offices of Lambton Cokeworks in the 1980s with piles of coke outside the window.

Three photographs of Lambton Cokeworks being demolished in the mid 1980s.

Jack Moore (far right in this picture) was chief engineer at Lambton Cokeworks. Here is a selection of photographs from the 1960s and 70s showing Jack and his workmates.

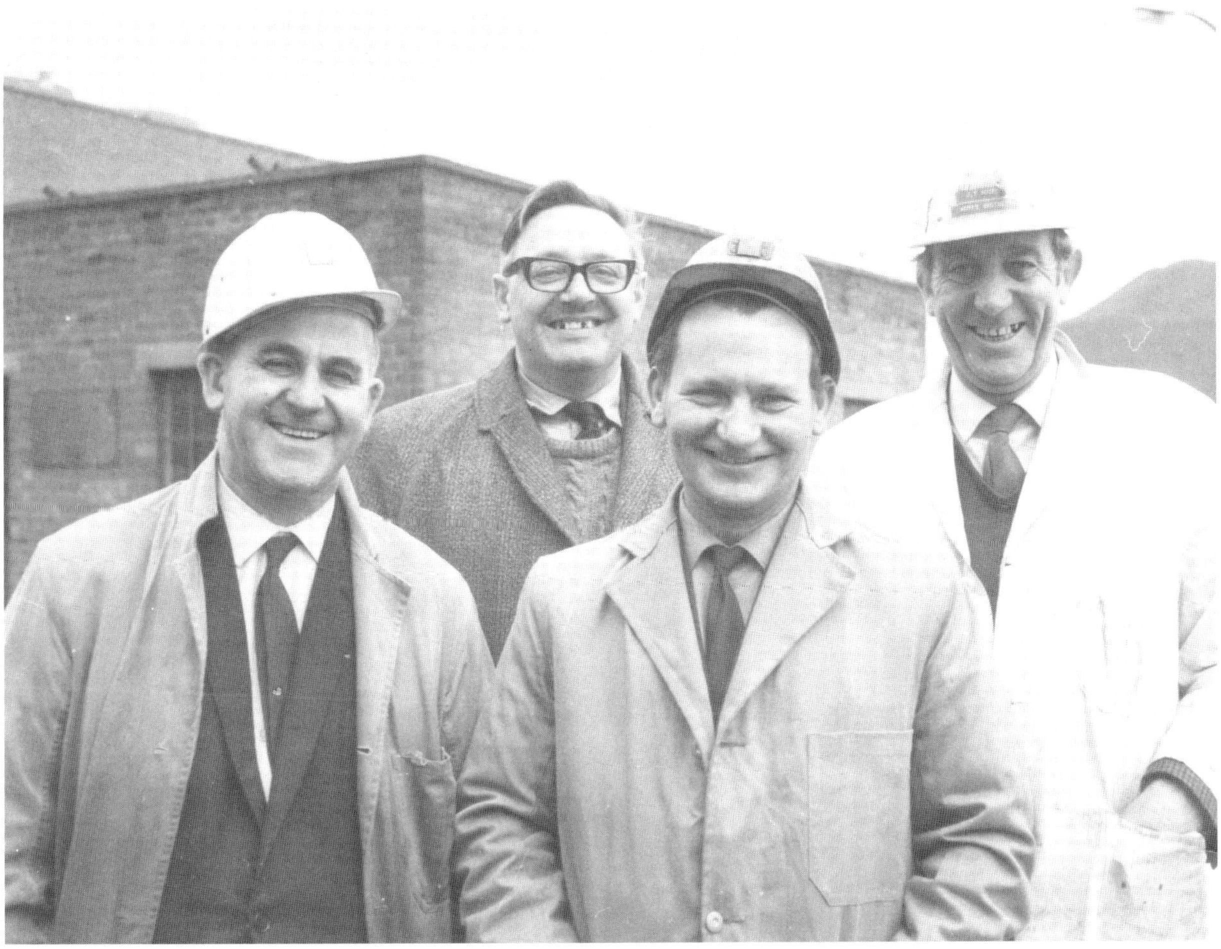

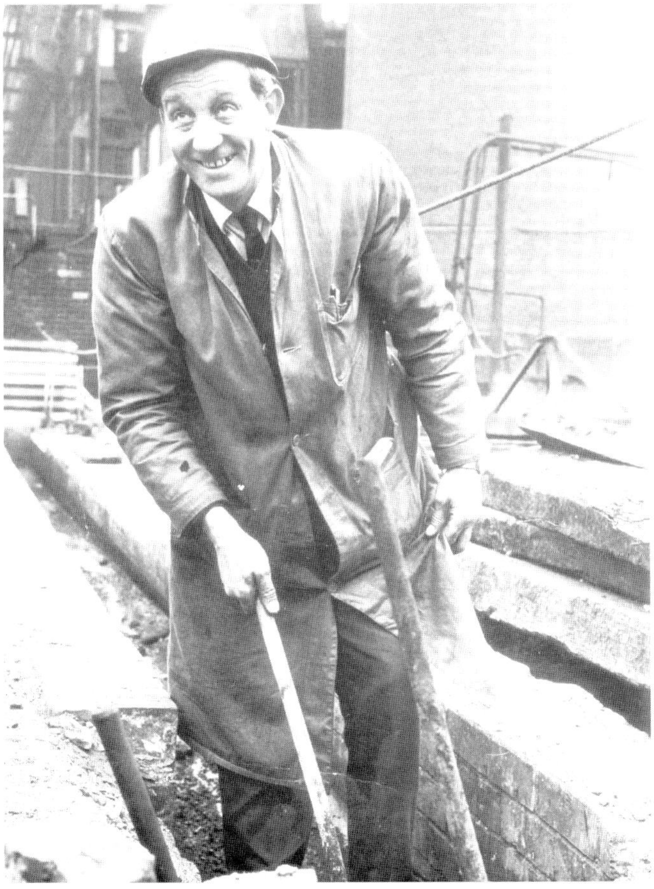

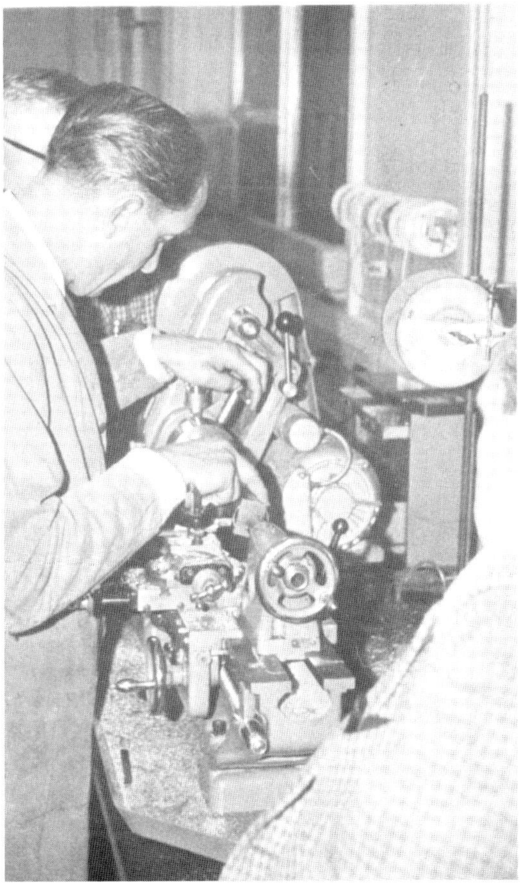

Lambton Cokeworks in its heyday. In 1974 the Chairman of the National Coal Board, Derek J. Ezra, predicted a bright future for the Cokeworks in the North East:

'Three of the North East's six NCB coking plants – Norwood, Derwenthaugh and Lambton – are pioneers of the technique developed locally by Board scientists in co-operation with our central research establishment, of blending coking coals of which Durham supplies a half of the national requirement. This ensures supplies of these coals, and of other coking reserves in the area, well into the next century, while also giving the market an eminently acceptable product.' Despite this optimism from Derek Ezra, Lambton Cokeworks was closed ten years later.

Left: A 4ft 2in gauge wagonway made of wood which was discovered buried beneath coal dust and slurry on the site of the former Lambton Cokeworks. The wagonway is believed to date from the late 1700s and was photographed in March 1996.

N Hyer's Clothing Factory

Two photographs of happy workers at N. Hyer's clothing factory in the 1960s.

Right: Shirley Shields and Florence Smith with Frank Hyer owner of N. Hyer's. The factory opened in 1945.

Wartime

It was announced by the Prime Minister, Neville Chamberlain, over the radio that Britain and Germany were at war in September 1939. Our whole lives changed because it affected everybody and everything. It was a new way of living and working and, dare I say it, discipline.

At Preston Hospital there was a lot of activity with sandbagging around important parts of the building, entrances etc. All windows during the war had to be covered at night so as not to show any lights in case there were enemy planes about or an air-raid was in progress. Everyone was issued and fitted with a gas mask that had to be carried around with you always in case of gas attacks by the enemy.

Above: Lena Cooper (far left back row) with staff and medics from one of the wards at Preston Hospital, North Shields (note the sandbags background) around 1939.

Some people were helped to make air-raid shelters in the middle of their gardens. We had air-raid wardens on constant duty because nobody knew just when a raid by the enemy would occur. If there was an air-raid warning given then everyone had to get to the shelters as quickly as possible. It was a bit frightening for children and for the elderly. They had to stay there until the 'all-clear' signal was given. Sometimes this meant spending all night in the shelter – not much fun! Eventually, we had a sing-song or some kind of guessing game; anything we could think of to make us forget where we were and why.

Right: An advert for the building of Air Raid Shelters, September 1939.

A.R.P.

Have Your Air Raid Shelter Soundly Constructed By The Firm Of Repute

Who are Contractors to H.M. Office of Works, War Office and Local Authorities.

The firm which knows what is required to comply with regulations.

F. W. GOODYEAR & SON,
60, CLAYPATH,
DURHAM.   Tel. 120.

It was the same sort of activities at Preston Hospital where I was at the time. Children were taken to shelters accompanied by nurses to look after them. However, a lot of the servicemen patients were unable to be moved so all lighting in the wards was subdued and nurses kept watch. Such relief when the all-clear was sounded. Everyone felt the pressure. When we nurses got a day off it felt in one way a relief for 24 hours but in another feeling it was like 'running away when we should be on duty.'

We had air-raid wardens at home and they had to ensure that no lights of any kind were visible from outside our homes or any building that was in use at the time. Even when an air-raid was over and we got the 'all-clear' signal the blackout situation remained. Our only consolation, if there was one, was that we knew that the whole country was also having to put up with these conditions and usually facing greater danger than we were.

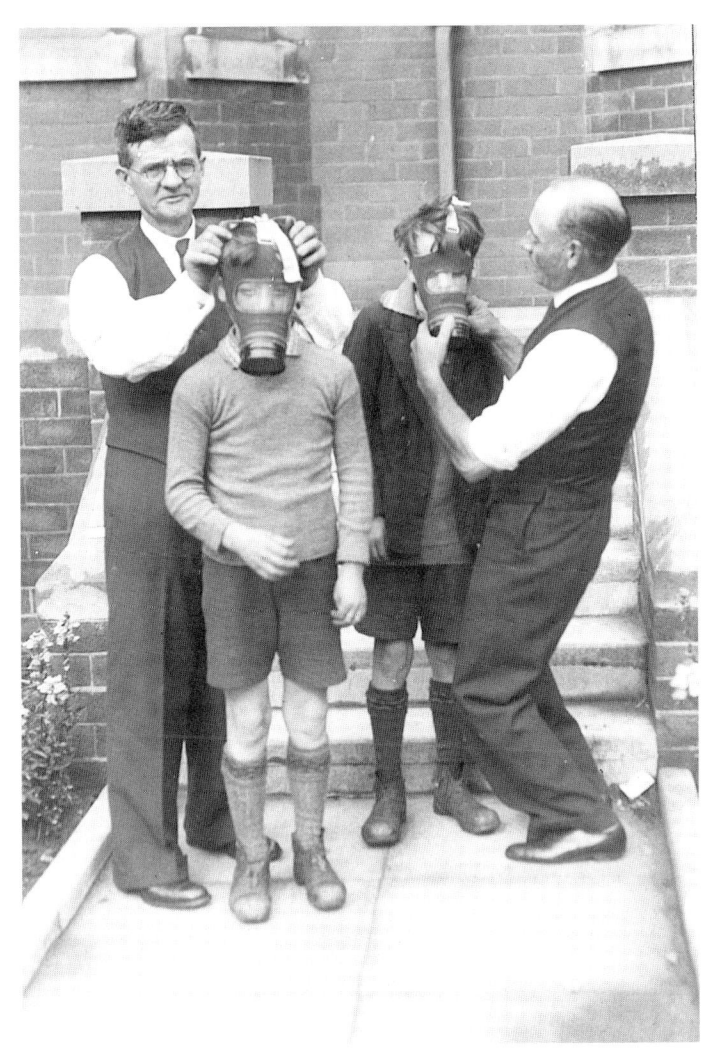

Right: Trying out gas masks at the start of the war.

OFFICIAL INSTRUCTIONS ISSUED BY THE MINISTRY OF HOME SECURITY

GAS ATTACK

HOW TO PUT ON YOUR GAS MASK

Always keep your gas mask with you – day and night. Learn to put it on quickly. **Practise wearing it.**

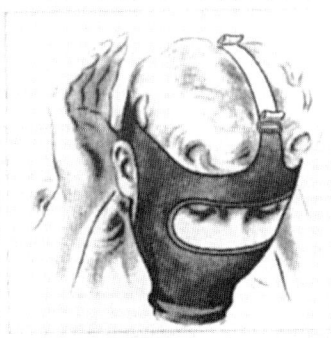

1. Hold your breath. 2. Hold mask in front of face, with thumbs inside straps.
3. Thrust chin well forward into mask, pull straps over head as far as they will go.
4. Run finger round face-piece taking care head-straps are not twisted.

Official instructions on how to put on your gas mask.

35

Food Rationing made front page news on 2nd November 1939.

Rationing of food started as early as four months after the declaration of war, with bacon, butter and sugar being the first goods on ration. Meat was rationed in March then tea, cooking fats and margarine in about July. Most other foods were gradually added to rationing. It was a difficult job trying to make your rations last. Of course we were issued with ration books and we had to use these coupons when buying our allotted ration of any foods. I think the food rationing went on until 1954 and I'm pretty sure that I still have in my 'archives' my old ration book. We were also all given books of clothing coupons.

The food rationing was at first very difficult to live with but on reflection it was probably better for us health-wise. We could not even imagine how dried egg powder could ever replace a fresh egg but like everything we got used to it. Dried egg was best used in baking or puddings and then it was more acceptable but only just!

Posters such as this encouraged everyone to make the most of their food during the war.

The government of the day launched a 'Dig for Victory' campaign and people were encouraged to dig up their flowerbeds and grow vegetables. People living in the country were better off for this purpose because they had more space and also access to berries, mushrooms and other wild foods that town-dwellers did not have.

As a result of this campaign we were able to have fresh vegetables grown in our own gardens and this was very acceptable to us country folk. We all had to survive and keep healthy as best we could. Even people at home had to make some contribution to the war-effort.

I have to admit I was never able to accept dried egg powder for any meal that I prepared so I usually avoided recipes in which it was required. I think the equivalent to one fresh egg was one level tablespoon of egg powder plus two level tablespoons of water. I think they had to be mixed together and then stand for five minutes until the powder had absorbed all the moisture then beaten with a fork, removing any lumps.

OFF THE ROAD —
but you can still get
RINGTONS TEA

BY instruction of the Ministry of Transport, the familiar Ringtons Vans have had to be taken off the road.

You can, however, still get Ringtons Tea, through specially-appointed distributing Agents.

Contact your Agent NOW, so as to ensure supplies of your favourite blend of Ringtons Tea in the new rationing period commencing July 25th. You will find the Quality and Flavour of Ringtons Tea still the best value obtainable.

Should you have any difficulty in obtaining supplies, send a post-card to the address below for name of your nearest Agent.

The new selling plan applies to all Ringtons Products... Tea, Coffee, Coffee Essence, Cocoa and Baking Powder.

RINGTONS, LTD., Tea Merchants,
Head Office: Algernon Road, Newcastle-on-Tyne, 6.

A wartime advert for this well known tea company.

John Tiplady during the Second World War.

The egg powder could be added dry to a recipe for plain cakes or puddings, mixing with the other dry ingredients but, when liquid was added to the mixture, two tablespoons extra per dry egg had to be allowed. Funnily, I could cope with everything else in the rationing scheme of things but not dried egg powder.

Fortunately, there were much more serious things to cope with than this so it was soon relegated to the bottom of my 'action list.' Little did we know how long the war would go on. Some people reckoned it would be over by Christmas. We could not have envisaged that it would be well into 1945 before peace was declared.

George Tiplady during the Second World War.

Vera Tiplady (née Bell) in uniform on 29th May 1943.

South Street, Bankhead, celebrates Victory in Europe after the Second World War.

People

Joan Cresswell in Fence Houses in 1958. Behind her is John Harland and in the pram is Thomas Harland.

Sadie Slack with her Grandma, Sally Dawson on Lambton Rec in 1940.

Sadie Slack, Stella Blackburn and Nora Blackburn on Lambton Rec in August 1955.

Lambton miner Billy Elliott walking his dog between the wars.

A group of soldiers on leave during the First World War with their dogs in Fence Houses.

Bob Minto with his friend Tosh Storey in the Broadway, Houghton-le-Spring, visiting Houghton Feast around 1984. In the background is the Britannia public house.

Albert Ellison, standard bearer of the Dubmire Branch of the Royal British Legion.

Right: Jack Glendening Johnson in his First World War uniform in late 1917. On his peaked cap is the General Service Coat of Arms badge of the Labour Corps, worn until late 1918 when it was replaced by one depicting a piled pick, rifle and shovel. He is wearing a leather 1914 pattern belt that was issued at the start of the war when there was insufficient webbing equipment available and was retained by many support units such as the Labour Corps. The Labour Corps was created in 1917 to bring together the diverse range of labour used by the army. Its duties included road and railway building and repair; loading and unloading ships; moving stores and ammunition; and burial duties. Soldiers of the Labour Corps were of a lower medical classification than those in front lines due to age, illness or previous wounds that made them unfit for normal duty.

Albert Ellison was chosen to represent the Dubmire Branch of the British Legion and the Northern Division at the funeral of Lord Louis Mountbatten. Here is his account of that day, the events leading up to it and his feelings concerning it:

'When I received the news that I had been selected for such a role I was filled with a mixture of pride and humility, conscious of the great honour that had been bestowed upon me and my branch and also of the tragedy and loss of the occasion. I travelled to London by train on the Monday preceding the funeral and arrived at the Milford Court Hotel. At the hotel I tried to get as much sleep as possible before awakened at the pre-arranged time of 3 am. I dressed and with other standard bearers boarded a bus that took is through the silent streets of the city to Horse Guards Parade for the rehearsal of the funeral the following day. We marched down Whitehall – the darkness and stillness adding to the poignancy of the situation. Near at hand we could hear the bands playing as we paced out steps to ensure that our movements in the procession the next day were executed to precision. As London slept we perfected our tribute to a great man, practising the lowering of our standards until the marshals were satisfied, we were suitably proficient. After receiving more instructions we went back to the hotel.

'The day of the funeral dawned and we were up at 6.30 am polishing shoes and brasses. Once more we arrived at Horse Guards Parade but this time the scene was one of bright sunshine that glinted off row upon row if uniforms. The crowds started to swell, with policemen stationed along the route at points only a few yards apart. We marched over the same ground we had covered before but this time we were being watched not just by a nation but by the entire world. As we stood with our standards an incident occurred that will stay in my mind for ever. The air had been very still but as the coffin bearing Lord Mountbatten passed, the standards were caught by the wind and began to flutter uncontrollably. Yet, as soon as the coffin moved on, the standards once again became still as the wind dropped. Before I left London I bought a book that traced the life of Lord Mountbatten and I asked the other standard bearers to sign their names in it – providing me with a reminder of the day we said farewell to a noble and greatly-mourned man.'

Entertainment

In the years before the Second World War if we could borrow or earn cash we went to the local picture house to see a film. The entrance fee for us young ones was threepence (in the pre-decimalisation days). After the show we could call at the local fish shop and get a pennyworth of chips to eat on the way home. If we could afford another tuppence it became fish and chips.

The Miners' Hall just over the station railways lines (to the left) used to get some wonderful shows on stage. Different companies would produce plays there for the general public to come and see. Of course they had to charge people for entrance to the show. One of my friends, whose father was chauffeur to a local 'big name' in the mining business, was able to go to see these shows and the following night would sit at her doorstep and tell us 'poorer' friends the whole show performance. We young folk loved to hear all about it because in those hard up days it was such a joy for us and it lifted our future possibilities for getting out of being 'broke'. We lived in hope that our efforts to do well would succeed.

Something different happened for young people in the early 1930s. The local newspaper *The Northern Echo* was always concerned about the well being of youngsters and started a children's club called the Nig Nog Ring hosted by an 'Uncle Mac and Uncle Ernest'. The words 'nig and nog' were Durham vernacular for boy and girl. The club became an enormous success and even produced their own local entertainment groups who often would perform for the people. I was a member of the Nig Nogs, along with many friends. It was fun. There were also benefits such as reductions in newspaper adverts if you were a member. We all got a round, blue badge bearing the word 'hullo' in the middle to prove we were indeed members.

We young folk would ask permission of parents if we could use the backyard for a concert. Once permission was given, with the usual warnings 'not to disturb neighbours', we would go ahead to plan the concert. First of all we had to find out who could sing; who could do acrobatics (simple stuff); who could tell a funny joke; and who could recite poems. The entrance fee to the backyard concert was one clean jam-jar. Usually the jam-jars were given to one of the mothers who made jam which at that time was invariably rhubarb.

A group of local musicians in the 1930s – John Tiplady is in the back row, second from the right. John Kelly, who was blind, is in the back row, far right.

A play at Fence Houses Secondary Modern School, 15th April 1949.

A lot of the time the entertainment enjoyed, as young people do, was to play tricks on grown ups. A favourite game was 'knocky-nine-doors' in which one of the group was chosen to knock on a certain front door and run to hide where the rest were out of sight. There had to be a brave youngster who would be one to peep out to see if the householder had answered the door. For some reason knocky-nine-doors was thought to be very funny. Remember we were all very young and did not have a lot of choice for entertainment so we had to devise our own. Bear in mind, if anyone was actually caught at this game then the whole group involved were told off by the householder and threatened with 'information would be given to the local policeman.' Personally, from my earliest schooldays I never joined in this particular activity. Even then I did not care for this as entertainment. In my mind at the time was a thought that to hurt anyone in any way – young or old – was never meant to give pleasure. My strict upbringing was being effective I guess.

With a portable organ plus organist the local chapels used to have a parade of their people go around the various streets, stopping now and then to sing their hymns. This happened annually on the 'anniversary' when the children said their 'piece' (a few lines of verse) which they had to learn by heart. This was in front of a full congregation and for some youngsters it was quite nerve-racking. They were later rewarded with a prize – usually a lovely book.

I was always nervous when it was my turn to say my piece, especially in front of all the people who knew me. I didn't want to let myself down but no-one ever had an inkling of the amount of courage it took for me to get to the end of my piece. Every year of course we each got a different piece to learn, ready for anniversary day. It was always supported and helped build up the funds for the chapel's annual outing and other activities, all for the benefit of the local children.

Comrades Club

Above: A Saturday night dance at the Comrades Club, Fence Houses. Included are: John Elliott, Dorothy Elliott, Annie Elliott, Tommy Garden and Bob Sanderson.

Left: At the bar in the Comrades Club – John Slack (Steward) and Eddy Bowman.

Right: Comrades Club, members on a Saturday night. Included are: Florrie Renshaw, Dorothy Elliott, Eddy Bowman, George & Shirley Shields.

Burnside Club

Dancing at Burnside Workingmen's club are Jack and Joyce Moore (right).

More dancing at Burnside Club. This time John Elliott is dancing with daughter-in-law Dorothy.

Members in Burnside Club in the 1930s – John Elliott, Bill Elliott and Clayton Lynn.

Days To Remember

A leek show in the Dun Cow around 1958. Standing, left to right: Kelly Besford, Jack Glowyne, Tommy Renshaw, George Greener, Reg Hall Snr, Neil Coulson. Sitting: Kit Scott, Reg Hall Jnr, Jack Bowery, Jim Jordan and Anne Jordan.

The Jolly Boys at Fence Houses Comrades Club stage a 'mock' wedding around 1950. Included in the photographs are: Mr & Mrs Ashman, Pop Martin, Trot Dixon, Bill Garden, Frank Dobson, Jack Garden, Tom Garden, Pop Martin (Snr), Mr Todd, Mr Weeks, Albert Garden, Mr Howe, Kelly Besford, George Besford, Norman Bolton and Jock McNeil (the 'bride').

Dubmire Workmen's Club Jolly Boys' Christmas party in 1951. Front row: Jigger Bainbridge, George Barker, Dick Eyre, Jackie Bainbridge, Jimmy Poulter, Jack McDermot. Second row: Tommy Bainbridge, Mickey Bainbridge, Dave Hann, Davy Jones, Levi Jones, Freddie Greenwell, Billy Todd (Snr), Alf Hubbick. Third row: Ned Brown, Packle Caulfield, unknown, Jackie Cox, Jim Ellison, Tommy Rowe, Billy Patterson, Tommy Farrer, Bert Edwards, W.P. Ellison, Diddler Bainbridge, Tessie Bennett, Ernie Robson (club steward), Slasher Naisbit. Fourth row: unknown, Cassler Brown, Billy Wrighton, Jonty Bainbridge, Fred Patterson, Tommy Brown, unknown, Herbie Curry, Fred Ellison, Jack Bruce. Fifth row: Tot Collier, unknown, unknown, Leslie Naisbit, ? Jack, Joe Elliott, Charlie Veitch, Tommy Hudson, Douglas Greenwell, Ralph Lawton, Henna Bainbridge. Back row: Billy Lindsley, Dyker Dixon, Freddie Bilton, ? Ayre, Super Brown, Jimmy Veitch, ? Naisbit, unknown, George Davis, Fred Robson and Ray ?.

A Hyers staff party in 1955. In the middle of the ladies are the manager Mr W. Russel and owners Anthony and Frank Hyer.

The opening of the 1st British Legion Hut at Colliery Row in the 1930s.

A group of Fence Houses ladies in fancy dress in the 1930s at a gathering in St Andrew's Church Hall opposite Britannia Terrace (now the British Legion Club House).

Right: A group of Fence Houses ladies at a function at St Andrew's Church in the 1920s.

Left: Happy days on a Dubmire Workman's Club outing in the 1960s.

49

New Lambton Bowling Club in the 1950s. Included are: Ann Slack, Nora Blackburn, Ena Pratt, Elsie Martin, Gertie Oliver, Mary Dodds, Mrs Moore and Mrs Robinson.

A crowd at a Burnside football match in the 1940s. Included are: Billy Elliott Jnr, Fred Blunt, George Reay, John Elliott, Jimmy Martin, Mrs Reay, Mrs Pratt and Mrs Hall.

Above: Outside the Dun Cow around 1957. Left to right: Jack Dixon Jnr, Brian Dixon, Jim Smith, Marie Dixon, Dolly Dixon (landlady), Cyril Watson, Reg Hall Jnr, Jim Jordan, Jack Bowery, Reg Hall Snr, Billy Renshaw, Tommy Jobling, Jimmy Hewitt, Andrew McCall, Jack Dixon Snr (landlord), Tommy Renshaw, George Greener and Kit Scott.

Right: All smiles at a Lambton Cokeworks dinner around 1970s Joyce Moore is the centre of these three ladies.

Left: Members of Dubmire Leek Club around 1947. Jack Guy is on the left.

YMCA

Fence Houses YMCA football team, Winners of the Washington League Cup, 1950-51. Included are: Billy Robinson, Jack Bilton, George Watchman, Ritchie Green, George Shields, David Purvis, Wilson Watt, Sid Dresser, Miles Dowell, Jimmy Jarvis and Alfie Cairns.

Presentation day at Fence Houses YMCA for the Winners of the Washington League Cup.

A crowd gathers for the opening of the Fence Houses YMCA playing fields.

At the YMCA in 1950. Left to right: Jean Hartis, Sid Tresser, George Hakin, Joan Gorman, Ronnie Bainbridge, George Shields, Shirley Elliott and Dougie Brown.

Church & Chapel

When we lived in Woodstone Terrace I had to attend Lumley Thicks Chapel every Sunday as soon as I was able to go. It became a three times a day commitment. Usually I went with friends and we went alongside what was known then as Dryden's Farm and across the fields to the chapel. This route was really a short cut.

I remember the senior members of our chapel. There was Mr George Carr, Mr Ramshaw, Mr Turnbull and his son Eddie, and several others who we younger ones looked up to with respect

There was usually a Sunday School outing each year to some local seaside area. I don't remember being allowed to go on these trips with the chapel people. Most likely my grandparents were not able to give me any extra cash for the outing. Remember they were pensioners. I was so lucky to be fed and clothed without any 'gallivanting'. Looking back now I realise how good they were. Bless them!

After the death of my Grandma I was informed that I should be going to Burnmoor Church now as I had turned thirteen. I was confirmed at the church by the Bishop of Jarrow and became a regular churchgoer thereafter. The Minister at the church at that time, Reverend A.J. Gadd gave me a lovely reference to use when I applied to be a nurse some five years later.

In one corner of this church (bottom left hand side looking from inside the entrance) there stands a large marble statue of an angel. It is fantastic and I believe was given to the church by a wealthy local landowner from his own mansion some many years ago. The angel statue has to be seen to be believed.

I was married at St Barnabas Church, Burnmoor, by the Reverend Gadd in December 1941.

The wedding day of Margaret Hardy and Bob Minto on 30th May 1936. Here Margaret is walking towards St Barnabas Church, Burnmoor with her father, Tom Hardy, and bridesmaid, Emma Ridley.

Having just been married the now Mrs Margaret Minto with her husband Bob at Fence Houses Station waiting to go on her honeymoon on 30th May 1936. The young girl is Emma Ridley. The name of the teenage lad is unknown.

Outside Lambton Primitive Methodists Chapel in 1960 are: John Tiplady, Gayner Tiplady, Annie Pratt, John Slack and Sadie Slack.

Janet Hamilton with her nephew in 1965 on the day of his Christening at St Andrew's Church, Chilton Moor.

Shirley Elliott and George Shields on their wedding day at Burnmoor Church in 1955. They are getting into a Bain's Taxi. Ambrose Bain was a local greengrocer and taxi driver.

Women's Groups

Above: A group of WI ladies from Fence Houses after the Second World War.

Left: Mary Hardy (ex school teacher – Chilton Moor school) being presented with a bouquet of flowers for her 90th birthday by Mrs Evelyn Berriman on behalf of the WI in 1981.

Founder members of Fence Houses WI in 1992.

Members of Fence Houses WI with Miss Hardy in the front row, right, in 1992.

A group of WI women and their families from Fence Houses at a Christmas party at the original YMCA building in Lambton Lane (near the station) in 1941.

A group of ladies at a dinner either in the old Church Hall at Chilton Moor or the original YMCA building along Lambton Lane (on the site where the new houses called the Sidings have been built) around 1945. The ladies were celebrating the end of the war during which time they were part of the group promoting the benefits of 'National Savings' for the war effort.

Sport

John Harland at Lambton School sports day at Burnmoor cricket field in 1961. Burnmoor Church is in the background.

Also at the Lambton School sports day in 1961 were Margaret Harland and Edna Cotcher.

Fence Houses Swimming team – Winners of a life saving trophy in a Northumberland and Durham competition in the late 1940s. The team were: Jimmy Richardson, Hazel Smith, Mr Bland, Shirley Elliott and Jack Weatley.

These three photographs were taken at Burnmoor Cricket and Tennis Club ground some time in the mid 1950s. Every year the club hosted a tennis tournament that attracted a large number of entries. Up to 18 courts could be marked out on the cricket field and used for the tournament that lasted for a complete week and can be seen on the bottom photograph. In the background is the old school building that is now occupied by Burnmoor Cricket Club. The Tennis Club has been in existence for nearly 100 years but there is some difficulty in determining from records as to the exact date when it was formed. These photographs were supplied by Mrs Anne Sowerby who still lives in the village and is still associated with the Tennis Club.

Football

Above: New Lambton School football team, 1952. Standing, left to right: Ray Pratt, Peter Morris, Brian Dixon, Billy Elliott, Tommy Gilbert, Ernie Hubbard, Terry Renshaw. Sitting: Mr Hunter (teacher), George McCafferty, Billy Atkinson, John Jackson, Mr Nicholson (headmaster), Alan Richardson, David Harbron and Mr Bolt (teacher).

Right: New Lambton Junior School football team, 1950.

Left: Woodlea Junior School football team, 1983-84. Back row, left to right: Steven Waites, Craig Fisher, Scot Pringle, Gordon Robson, Grant Cockburn, Paul Fletcher, Neil Conn. Front row: Mr Yates, Mark Green, John Walsh, Andrew Slack, Andrew Williamson, Ian Robson and Ian Storey.

Fence Houses Junior football team, 1953. Back: Mr Kirkbride (headmaster). Second row: Tommy McKitten, Ralph Oliver, Harry Thompson, Norman Walker, Harry Graham, Peter Morris, Jackie Bainbridge. Front row: Fred Hall, Derek Pimlett, Billy Watson (captain), Brian Williams and Brian Lister.

Dubmire School Under 11s football team, 1954-55. Mr Greenwell (headmaster) left; Mr Smith (sports master) centre, Mr Reid (teacher) right. Back row: A. Cummings, D. Crocket, A. Parton, J. Ayre, J. McNeil, J. Slack, B. Bainbridge. Front row: C. Guy, J. Tall, C. Richardson, D. Tall and G. Tiplady.

Bankhead football team around the 1930s. Back row: Lockie Todd, George Passmore, Pop Elliott, J. Bilton, Eddie Charlton, Wilf Hill. Front row: Bob Passmore, Benny Mossman, unknown, unknown, Tucker Richardson and Kelly Besford.

Lumley Juniors, 1949-50. Back row, left to right: J. Nightingale, Joe Walt, Mickey Wilson, George Shields, Ed Wilson, unknown, unknown. Front row: Mintoe Carr, Ed Stoker, Vince Woodhead and Stephen Cairns.

Lambton Cokeworks football team in 1935. This team must have had a successful season as a cup is on display.

Two photographs of a Burnside charity football match around 1950. The game was played between a team of married men and a team of single men. The mascot was Bertie Ord (far right) and the referee and guest of honour was Newcastle United star, Frank Brennan (far left).

The single men team. Included are: Neil Coulson, George Besford, Benny Mossman and Mr Blackbird.

The married men team. Included are: Joe Spence, Joe Thompson, Frankie Hope, John Elliott, Joe Spence, Robert Besford, Mr Hall and Dr George.

Cricket

Above: Two photographs of Tom Hardy in his Burnmoor cricket days before the Second World War. Tom opened the batting for Burnmoor in those days.

Left: Burnmoor cricketers in 1936 after a winning a trophy. Tom Hardy is at the front of the group on the ground to the left.

Joe Linsley with his wife Olive and Geoff Atkinson on a warm summer's day outside Burnmoor Cricket Club around 1954. This was at a time before the bar was built and the old entrance is in the background. The land adjoining St Barnabas Church is the Burnmoor Cricket field where the game has flourished for well over 100 years. Blunt, Woodhouse, Bulmer, Clark, Hardy, Forster, Gelson and Linsley are some of the well known names of cricketers from the 1940s and '50s. The tradition still lives on today with Joe Linsley's son, Ian, who is involved in many important management roles of the modern club, following his retirement from the playing side.

Left: Joe Linsley and his son Ian taken on the only occasion that father and son played together for Burnmoor Cricket Club in the Durham Senior League. On this occasion, in 1964, Ian (aged 16) and his dad Joe (aged 48) played against Sunderland. It was Joe's last game before retiring from the side.

Burnmoor Cricket Team in the 1940s. Back row: T. Kirby, T. Combey, J.J. Swinney, M. Raine, J. Shurben, H. Jackson, G. Atkinson, P. Walton, E. Kirtley, J.W. Linsley, R.B. Dodds, W. Lee, P.S. Clark, J.H. Swinney, R. Thompson, W. Edger. Middle row, seated: G. Linsley, T. Allison, J. Gelson, E. Clark, T. Browell. Front row, sitting/kneeling: J. Gelson, F. Richardson, R. Attis.

Chilton Moor cricket team, Durham Coast League Joint Champions in 1962. Back row, left to right: Bill Oliver, Frank Hood, Harry Vasey, Jim Baker, Brian Roxby, Bill Edger. Front row: unknown, unknown, Jim Wilkinson, John Elliott, A. Smith and unknown.

Netball

Above and left: Two Fence Houses netball teams from 1931. On the right in the team above is Miss Woodward (headmistress). On the team to the left are the following girls: Hilda Ramshaw, Elsie Hall, Polly Dawson, Nora Young and Doris Reed.

Lambton School netball team, Champions in 1947. Back row, left to right: Hazel Smith, Betty Bolton, Shirley Elliott, Ivy Burn. Front row: Marie Dixon, Joan Gilbert and Sheila Maxie.

People

The Burrows family from the Bankhead area of Fence Houses. Back row: Christopher. Second row, left to right: Phoebe, Margaret (mother) née Matthews, Joshia, Joshia Guy, Beatrice. Front row: Louise, Methuen, Ethel and Jonathan.

Left: Four members of the Elliott family. On the right is Jack the father of three sons, from left: Billy, John and Ernie.

Sadie Slack, Billy Blackburn and Nora Blackburn at the Rec in the 1950s.

Billy Blackburn with two lads and a dog at the Rec around 1950.

Mr & Mrs Hamilton outside the front door of their house at 32 Avon Crescent, Chilton Moor around the 1940s.

John and Sally Dawson with their grandaughter, Sadie, in 1941.

Annie Pratt at the Rec in the 1940s.

Shopping

In the 1930s there was a greater number of shops in the local area than there is now.

A general confectioner's shop was built on to the bottom of Finchale Terrace at Sixth Pit. If I remember correctly it was owned by a family called Langtons. It was later used for other businesses and is now a dwelling house.

At the end of the first block of Gill Crescent North there was a general shop owned by the Dawson family. This also soon became a dwelling house.

Towards the bottom end of the second block of Gill Crescent North a family firm of Metcalf's had a grocery store. Then Tindale's butcher shop and Graham's general dealers.

Knights had a general dealers shop at the top end of the second block of Gill Crescent South and I remember a private house front window showed confectionery for a while.

At the corner end of Morton Grange Crescent, Bains had a general dealers shop – a family business.

There was an off-licence shop at the bottom end of South Crescent (opposite the Memorial for the First World War). A few doors along was Hardy's men's hairdressers. Then further along was Fennel's ladieswear shop, the Fish Shop, then Gallon's Groceries – which was later a tea-room plus ice cream – the newspaper shop owned by Fred Towers then the Crescent Picture House.

The well known newsagent's shop belonging to Mr F. Tower. The shop was adjacent to the Palace Picture House, also known as the Crescent.

On the opposite side of the road was Morton Crescent and the Meadow Dairy at the end of the first block of Morton Crescent. At the beginning of Morton Crescent (first block) lived Tommy Anderson the 'Yeast Man'. He delivered yeast with his pony and trap.

At the beginning of the second block of Morton Crescent about two houses up was a front window demonstration of antique-type furniture – I think the name of the firm was Welbourns. A few doors up was a bicycle shop for various items and accessories and outside in their front yard was a petrol pump.

Further up the same block was a very popular butchers shop (known for years as Wilkinson's) then a chemist shop. Two doors further up was a confectioner's shop (for years run by the Pratt family), then a shop selling china goods was next. The most popular shop in my mind was Pratt's Fish Shop at the end of Morton Crescent.

Opposite the fish shop, at the top end of Co-operative Terrace was the Fence Houses branch of the Chester-le-Street Co-operative Society. This incorporated all the different departments which had their own separate door entrances (before reorganisation).

Over the Fence Houses Station railway lines was Station Avenue on each side of the main road and each side had the odd confectioner's shop. At Bankhead (left of the main road) there was a fish shop and a bakery (later Winship's) and further towards Colliery Row there was a newsagents and the Post Office, plus another shop that is now a dwelling house. Roxby's men's hairdressers was also on that side of the street. On the other side of the main street, George Graham Stores were positioned. Then the main road turns left at Colliery Row and leads down to Houghton-le-Spring.

Houghton was a good shopping place for local people and it was even a walkable distance. In Houghton there was Woolworths, Stone's (pork butchers), Wheatley's (confectioners), newsagents, fruit and vegetable shops, Pallisters (household goods), Doggarts (clothing etc) and others.

Wheatley's Toffee Works in Houghton around 1950.

Local people also did their shopping in Chester-le-Street. At the bottom end of the town's main street was the Chester-le-Street Co-operative Society Stores, a vast building. On the opposite side of the street was Woolworth's and Doggarts. Midway up the street, I remember a store called Murdoch's that sold household goods and clothing.

It will be noticed, I expect, that I have not mentioned any public houses in the area. The reason being that they would need a whole book!

Mining Memories

Lambton Miners' Lodge Banner in the early 1950s. Standing, far left is George Gaunt, seventh left is Jack Middlemass, far right is Inky Passmore. Sitting, far left is Billy Strafford.

Durham Miners' Gala in the late 1950s. In the centre is Tommy Renshaw with Jack Craggs lighting a cigarette. Far right is Michael Dowell.

In The Office

I started working for the National Coal Board in 1955, in the Mechanisation Department situated at that time in Stockton Road, Sunderland. My immediate 'Boss' – the one I actually worked for – was George Renwick who was in charge of the mechanisation of the local mines. Machinery was taking over a lot of the hard back-breaking work of the miners. A mining revolution! He had a team of men to help organise and get this system working.

Then one morning the Senior Clerical Officer showed me an internal staff circular he had just received, asking for applications for a clerical vacancy in the Chairman's Office. Wow! The Chairman's Office at that time was in the National Coal Board Offices in Milburn House, Newcastle. He suggested that I should apply for the vacancy (in his view this position was 'top of the tree'). After a lot of persuasion and careful thought, I finally applied for the vacancy. It was one of the best decisions I ever made. I was granted an interview and, when that special day arrived, I was almost a nervous wreck. But I got the job.

In those days I found it easier to park my car in Gateshead on open spare ground, then get a bus across the Tyne Bridge. It took only about five minutes to walk down from the bus stop to Milburn House near the Quayside.

The job itself was a very confidential one – I was privy to the sight of meeting papers which, at that time, contained some very secret information. I had to attach any relevant papers and minutes thereon to the new Board Papers, in order that the Chairman could quickly check any previous information on the particular subjects.

While still at Milburn House, and a short time after I started in the Chairman's office, the new Chairman, Dr William Reid took over. When we moved to Team Valley Trading Estate offices there were three of us who were Chairman's staff, his secretary, a typist and myself.

Lena Cooper (left) and Muriel Melville outside the Coal Board Offices at Team Valley Trading Estate in the 1960s.

When any Board meetings or special meetings were held in the Boardroom we were designated to serve coffee to all members in the meeting. Three of the many VIPs who visited Dr Reid were: Lord Robens – Chairman of the National Coal Board from 1961 to 1971, a strong character at the time. Dr Bronowski – the intellectual thinker, a quiet-voiced man, gentle mannered. Sam Watson – of the National Union of Mineworkers, Durham Area, a pleasant 'man of the people'.

We all loved Dr Reid. If there is such a person – he was the perfect boss. He was a gentleman, kind understanding, helpful, appreciative, hard-working, a very clever man and greatly respected. When he received the honour of a CBE Award, we were all so proud of him. Some time later, when he received his knighthood, I was so full of pride knowing that for a number of years I had the privilege of working for Sir William Reid.

Sam Watson with members of the Silksworth Lodge in the mid 1960s. Sam, who started at Boldon Colliery when he was fourteen, was elected Agent for the Durham Miners' Association in 1936. He served for twenty-seven years until he retired in 1963.

Streets & Backlanes

Above and left: A young Edith Hardy (daughter of Tom Hardy and niece to Miss Mary and Miss Margaret Hardy) at the rear of her aunt Mary's house at 17 Station Avenue North, Fence Houses. The date is 1941 – prior to the building of the Grange Estate.

Workers building Gregory Terrace, Fence Houses in the late 1940s. Included are: George Shields, Teddy Welsh and Billy Dresser.

Joyce Moore outside her home at Woodland Grange, Fence Houses in the 1950s. You can see Morton Crescent behind.

John and Sally Dawson, 32 Chapel Row, Lambton, in the 1940s.

Outside Redburn Cottages are Lilian Pringle (mother), Lilian Pringle (daughter), Doris Hunter (Tate) and Betty Pringle.

John Elliott at the New Lambton bowling green in 1949. Chapel Row is at the back.

George Shields with his nephew, Kevin Elliott, at 4A Railway Terrace, New Lambton in 1959.

John Dawson and John Slack at Chapel Row, Lambton, around 1950.

Shirley Elliott at Railway Terrace, New Lambton in 1950.

Mrs Gordon and Mrs Moore outside George Street, Bankhead, in the 1950s. Mrs Moore had a shop at the end of the street.

At Lambton allotments in 1961 are John Harland with his three sons John, Thomas and Graham. Bethal Chapel is in the background.

John Elliott and his dog in the back street of 4A Railway Terrace in the 1940s.

John Harland and Steve Stavers in Lambton in 1959.

Roy Curry at Finchale Filling Station in the winter of 1979.

John Elliott and Eddy Bowman in front of the Railway line, Fence Houses, in the 1950s.

Thanks for the Memories

Here are some final images of local people. I am sure the reader will recognise many of the faces, perhaps you might even see yourself!

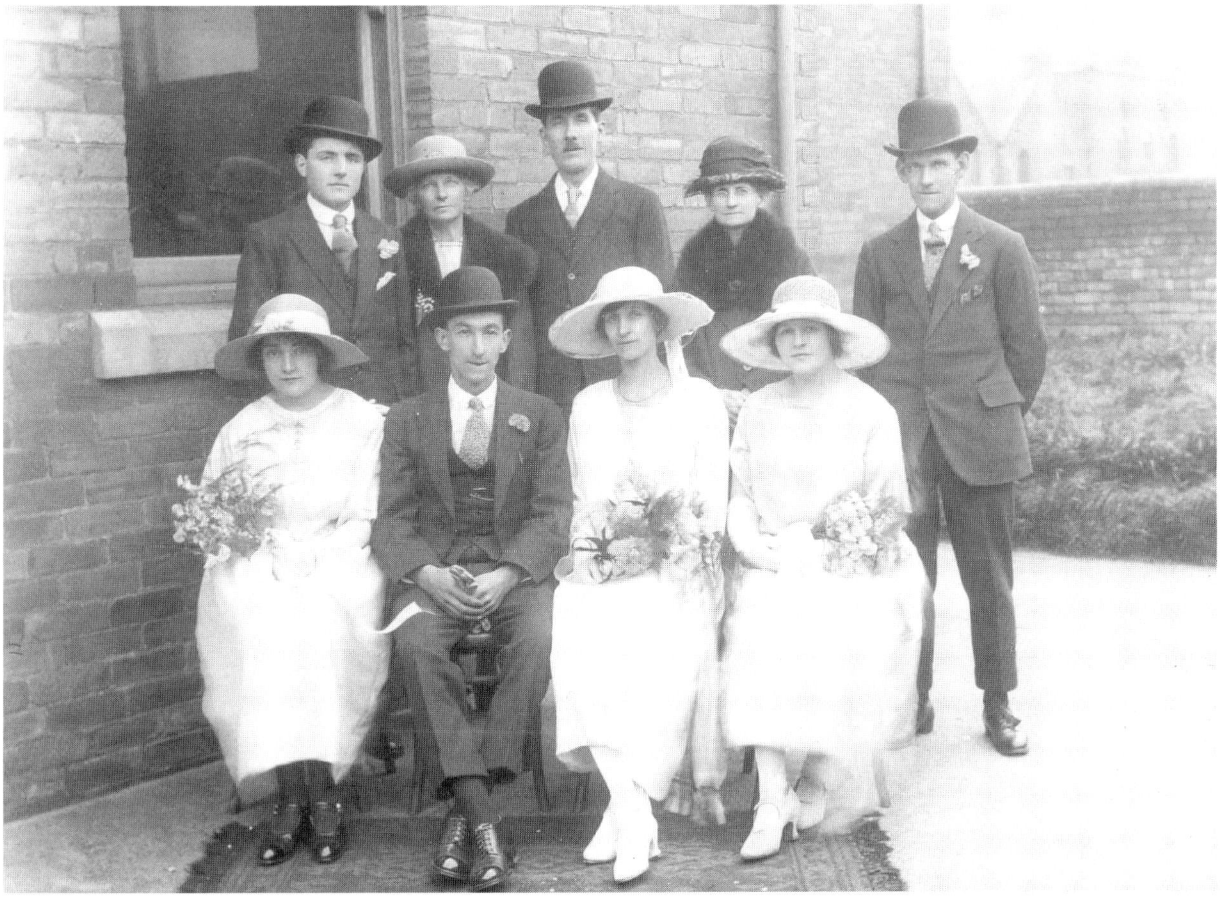

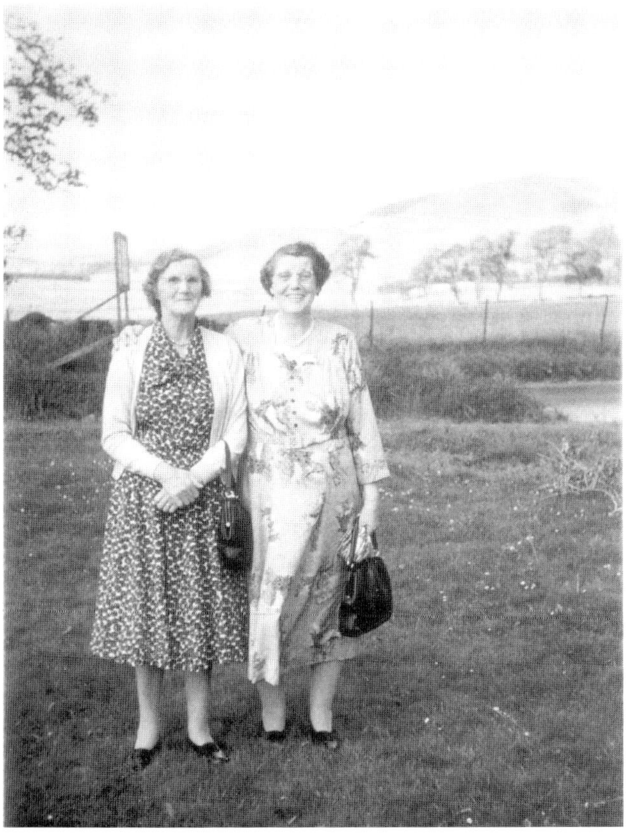

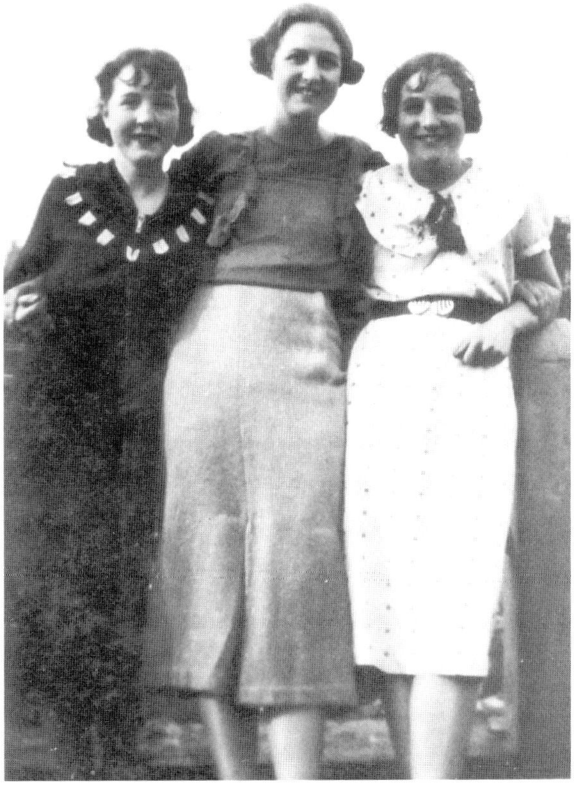

Also available from Summerhill Books

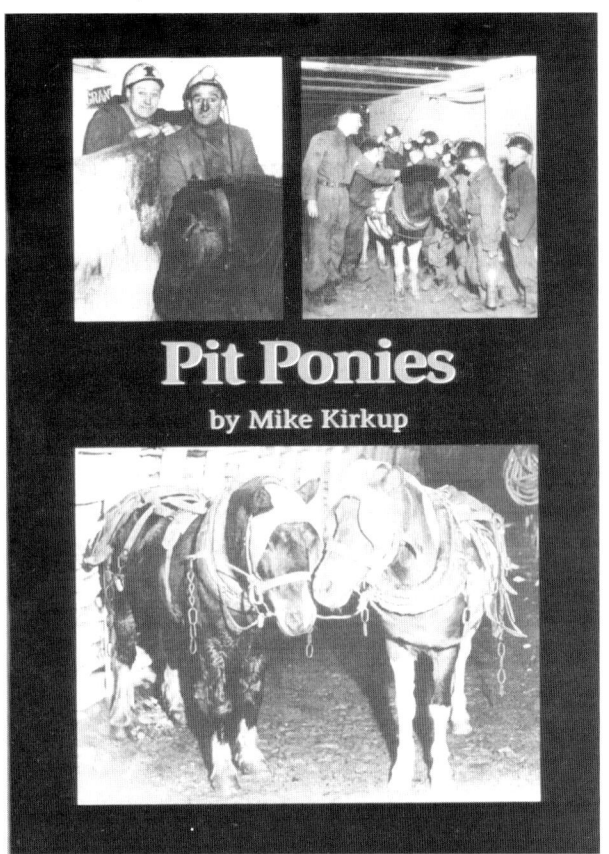

Pit Ponies

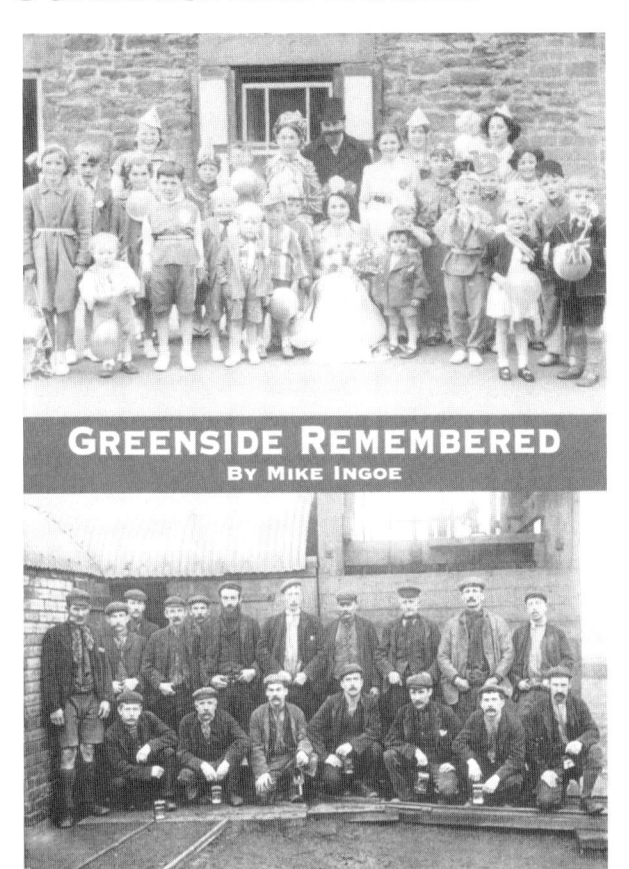

Greenside Remembered

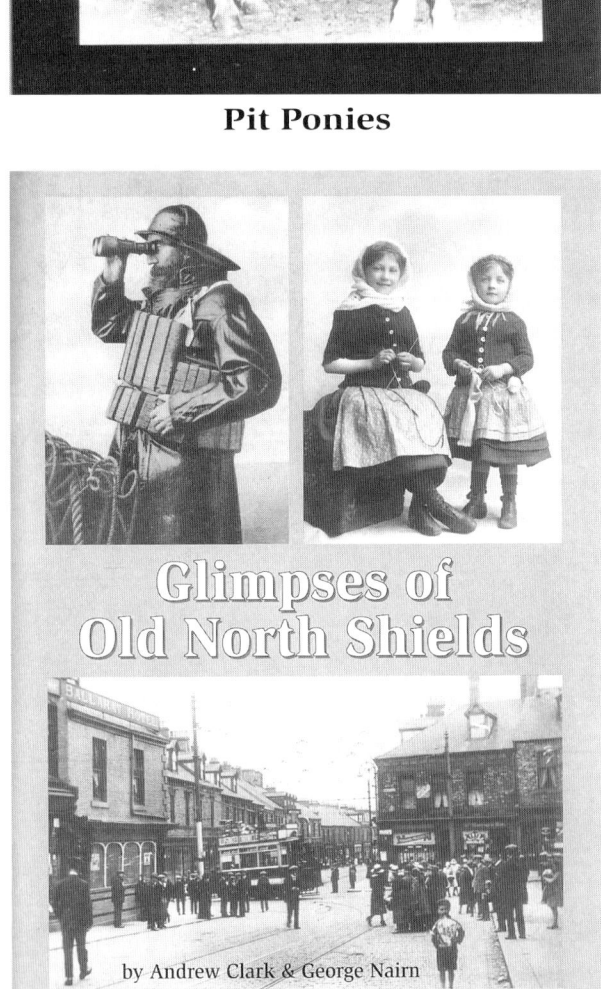

Glimpses of
Old North Shields

Glimpses of Tynemouth,
Cullercoats & Whitley Bay